THE KINDNESS PROJECT

A 30 DAY CHALLENGE WORKBOOK TO LIVING KIND

THIS BOOK BELONGS TO:

_____

DATE:_____

TODAY I CHOSE TO BE KIND
DAY 1

WRITE DOWN
HOW YOU
SHOWED
KINDNESS
TODAY
←---------

DRAW A PICTURE THAT REPRESENTS YOUR KIND ACT BELOW

TODAY I CHOSE TO BE KIND
DAY 2

WRITE DOWN
HOW YOU
SHOWED
KINDNESS
TODAY
←---------

DRAW A PICTURE THAT REPRESENTS YOUR KIND ACT BELOW

TODAY I CHOSE TO BE KIND
DAY 3

WRITE DOWN
HOW YOU
SHOWED
KINDNESS
TODAY
←---------

DRAW A PICTURE THAT REPRESENTS YOUR KIND ACT BELOW

TODAY I CHOSE TO BE KIND
DAY 4

WRITE DOWN
HOW YOU
SHOWED
KINDNESS
TODAY
←---------

DRAW A PICTURE THAT REPRESENTS YOUR KIND ACT BELOW

TODAY I CHOSE TO BE KIND
DAY 5

WRITE DOWN
HOW YOU
SHOWED
KINDNESS
TODAY
←---------

DRAW A PICTURE THAT REPRESENTS YOUR KIND ACT BELOW

TODAY I CHOSE TO BE KIND
DAY 6

WRITE DOWN
HOW YOU
SHOWED
KINDNESS
TODAY
←---------

DRAW A PICTURE THAT REPRESENTS YOUR KIND ACT BELOW

TODAY I CHOSE TO BE KIND
DAY 7

WRITE DOWN
HOW YOU
SHOWED
KINDNESS
TODAY
←---------

DRAW A PICTURE THAT REPRESENTS YOUR KIND ACT BELOW

TODAY I CHOSE TO BE KIND
DAY 8

WRITE DOWN
HOW YOU
SHOWED
KINDNESS
TODAY
←---------

DRAW A PICTURE THAT REPRESENTS YOUR KIND ACT BELOW

TODAY I CHOSE TO BE KIND
DAY 9

WRITE DOWN
HOW YOU
SHOWED
KINDNESS
TODAY
←---------

DRAW A PICTURE THAT REPRESENTS YOUR KIND ACT BELOW

TODAY I CHOSE TO BE KIND
DAY 10

WRITE DOWN
HOW YOU
SHOWED
KINDNESS
TODAY
←---------

DRAW A PICTURE THAT REPRESENTS YOUR KIND ACT BELOW

TODAY I CHOSE TO BE KIND
DAY 11

WRITE DOWN
HOW YOU
SHOWED
KINDNESS
TODAY

←---------

DRAW A PICTURE THAT REPRESENTS YOUR KIND ACT BELOW

TODAY I CHOSE TO BE KIND
DAY 12

WRITE DOWN
HOW YOU
SHOWED
KINDNESS
TODAY
←---------

DRAW A PICTURE THAT REPRESENTS YOUR KIND ACT BELOW

TODAY I CHOSE TO BE KIND
DAY 13

WRITE DOWN
HOW YOU
SHOWED
KINDNESS
TODAY
←---------

DRAW A PICTURE THAT REPRESENTS YOUR KIND ACT BELOW

TODAY I CHOSE TO BE KIND
DAY 14

WRITE DOWN
HOW YOU
SHOWED
KINDNESS
TODAY
←---------

DRAW A PICTURE THAT REPRESENTS YOUR KIND ACT BELOW

TODAY I CHOSE TO BE KIND
DAY 15

WRITE DOWN
HOW YOU
SHOWED
KINDNESS
TODAY
←---------

DRAW A PICTURE THAT REPRESENTS YOUR KIND ACT BELOW

TODAY I CHOSE TO BE KIND
DAY 16

WRITE DOWN
HOW YOU
SHOWED
KINDNESS
TODAY
←---------

DRAW A PICTURE THAT REPRESENTS YOUR KIND ACT BELOW

TODAY I CHOSE TO BE KIND
DAY 17

WRITE DOWN
HOW YOU
SHOWED
KINDNESS
TODAY
←---------

DRAW A PICTURE THAT REPRESENTS YOUR KIND ACT BELOW

TODAY I CHOSE TO BE KIND
DAY 18

WRITE DOWN
HOW YOU
SHOWED
KINDNESS
TODAY
←----------

DRAW A PICTURE THAT REPRESENTS YOUR KIND ACT BELOW

TODAY I CHOSE TO BE KIND
DAY 19

WRITE DOWN
HOW YOU
SHOWED
KINDNESS
TODAY
←---------

DRAW A PICTURE THAT REPRESENTS YOUR KIND ACT BELOW

TODAY I CHOSE TO BE KIND
DAY 20

WRITE DOWN
HOW YOU
SHOWED
KINDNESS
TODAY
←---------

DRAW A PICTURE THAT REPRESENTS YOUR KIND ACT BELOW

TODAY I CHOSE TO BE KIND
DAY 21

WRITE DOWN
HOW YOU
SHOWED
KINDNESS
TODAY
←---------

DRAW A PICTURE THAT REPRESENTS YOUR KIND ACT BELOW

TODAY I CHOSE TO BE KIND
DAY 22

WRITE DOWN
HOW YOU
SHOWED
KINDNESS
TODAY
←---------

DRAW A PICTURE THAT REPRESENTS YOUR KIND ACT BELOW

TODAY I CHOSE TO BE KIND
DAY 23

WRITE DOWN
HOW YOU
SHOWED
KINDNESS
TODAY
←---------

DRAW A PICTURE THAT REPRESENTS YOUR KIND ACT BELOW

TODAY I CHOSE TO BE KIND
DAY 24

WRITE DOWN
HOW YOU
SHOWED
KINDNESS
TODAY
←---------

DRAW A PICTURE THAT REPRESENTS YOUR KIND ACT BELOW

TODAY I CHOSE TO BE KIND
DAY 25

WRITE DOWN
HOW YOU
SHOWED
KINDNESS
TODAY
← - - - - - - - - -

DRAW A PICTURE THAT REPRESENTS YOUR KIND ACT BELOW

TODAY I CHOSE TO BE KIND
DAY 26

WRITE DOWN
HOW YOU
SHOWED
KINDNESS
TODAY
←---------

DRAW A PICTURE THAT REPRESENTS YOUR KIND ACT BELOW

TODAY I CHOSE TO BE KIND
DAY 27

WRITE DOWN
HOW YOU
SHOWED
KINDNESS
TODAY
←---------

DRAW A PICTURE THAT REPRESENTS YOUR KIND ACT BELOW

TODAY I CHOSE TO BE KIND
DAY 28

WRITE DOWN
HOW YOU
SHOWED
KINDNESS
TODAY
←---------

DRAW A PICTURE THAT REPRESENTS YOUR KIND ACT BELOW

TODAY I CHOSE TO BE KIND
DAY 29

WRITE DOWN
HOW YOU
SHOWED
KINDNESS
TODAY
←---------

DRAW A PICTURE THAT REPRESENTS YOUR KIND ACT BELOW

KINDNESS
CREATES
KINDNESS

TODAY I CHOSE TO BE KIND
DAY 30

WRITE DOWN
HOW YOU
SHOWED
KINDNESS
TODAY
←---------

DRAW A PICTURE THAT REPRESENTS YOUR KIND ACT BELOW

Printed in Great Britain
by Amazon